*Love Yourself
Before
Anyone Else*

Love Yourself Before Anyone Else

Charley Johnson

Copyright © 2024
Charley Johnson

Performance Publishing
McKinney, TX

All Worldwide Rights Reserved.

All rights reserved. No part of this publication may be reproduced, stored in a retrieval system or transmitted, in any form or by any means, electronic, mechanical, recorded, photocopied, or otherwise, without the prior written permission of the copyright owner, except by a reviewer who may quote brief passages in a review.

ISBN: 978-1-961781-79-5

Contents

Your Love 1
Saudade 4
Written in Stone 5
Cinguomania 8
Heartbreak #1 9
Lust 12
Heartbreak #2, What is Love? 13
Induratize 15
Meaning of Words 16
Tacenda 17
Things I Notice About You 18
Viridity 20
Assume 21
Fanna 23
I'm Sorry I'm Texting Again 24
Epiphany 26
Nothing But a Seed 27
Reverie 28
What "I Love You" Means 29
Philophobia 31
Blindly Led Off a Cliff 32
Filipendulous 35
By the Way… 36
Anagapesis 37
My Body not my Heart 38
Xenization 40

A Poem For You	41
Cafuné	43
Our Story	44
Onsra	47
Live, Laugh, Love?	48
Thanatophobia	49
Remember? Forget.	50
Athazagoraphobia	53
War of Nonsense	54
Anecdoche	56
Mr. No Name	57
Ilynga	59
Souls or Strings	60
Koi no yokan	62
Before and After	63
Toska	65
The Balloon of Your Love	66
Twitterpated	68
User Not Found	69
Lyssamania	72
Digging a Pit	73
Stardust	75
Flow or Run	76
Clysmic	77
Roses	78
Kalon	80
Can You Cry Underwater?	81
Orenda	83
What You Want Me For	84
Illecebrous	86

A Poem Written When He Was Around	87
Forelsket	89
Just Let Me Drown	90
Lisztomania	92
My Friend, Jim	93
L'appel du Vide	95
Grey Skies	96
Desiderium	99
I'm Not Perfect	100
Atelophobia	101
Poetry is Love	102
Fustian	104
More Than My Writing	105
Pulchritudinous	108
Can I Succeed?	109
Egonoia	111
Just Cry	112
Tears	115
Make a Wish	116
Lachrymose	117
Vocal Cords	118
Agathokakological	120
Bloody Hands	121
Bêtise	122
Patience With Love	123
Redamancy	125
Your Love 2- Self Love	126
Agape	129
What Is Love?	130

Your Love

H eat.
It's comforting.
The warmth from a fire.
The warmth from a hug.
Cozy blankets, fuzzy socks, hot sand.

Fire.
Fire is heat.
But not always comforting.
Flames rising tall, surrounded.
Smoke filling the air, suffocated.
Fire.

Your love is like fire.
Dangerous.
Harmful.
Painful.
It destroys everything in its path.
Destruction.

It once was like heat.
Safe.
Warm.
Loving.
All of that changed in seconds.

Love Yourself Before Anyone Else

That candle I lit for you broke.
And everything was set to flames.
Unbearable.
You hurt me.
Constantly.
The fire did damage.
You weakened me.

Your flames burned my structure.
I am unstable.
The slightest push makes a crack.
Cracks add up.
They result in a crumble.

And even after all of that.
Your memories are salvageable.
Your warmth.
Our shared laughs.
Our love.

It was ours.
I was building that house for us.
Us.
What we could have had.

Now I must rebuild it on my own.
For me.
There is no more us.
We were set to flames.
Burned.

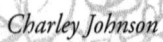

Charley Johnson

Our love to ashes.
Blown away with the wind.

I pick up shards of glass.
The glass from your candle.
Cutting my hands as I collect them.
You continue to hurt me.
It never ends.

Yet, I will not rid of your memory.
Those pictures, hoodies, jewelry, and glass will be saved.
Tucked away in a box.
Pushed away while I rebuild myself.

You will always be there.
A distant thought.
A memory.

I choose to remember only your candle.
Not your flames.
Your heat.
Not your fire.

Saudade

[souˈdädə]
noun

"A nostalgic longing to be near again to something or someone that that has been loved and then lost"

"The love that remains."

Charley Johnson

Written in Stone

I once wrote out my feelings.
The feelings I had for you.
I wrote them on a napkin.
Not the most convenient, but in writing.

Then you got with her.
I was filled with hurt.
Rage.
I tore up that napkin.
Those feelings, destroyed.
Yet something didn't feel right.
Those feelings were still there.

I wrote out my feelings.
The feelings I had for you.
This time on paper.
I kept it in my back pocket.
Close to me.
The way I wish you were.

I saw you and her holding hands,
sharing hugs,
the way you smiled at her.
I tore up the paper.
And with it, my feelings for you.
Gone.

Yet, the thought of you remained.

I wrote out my feelings.
The feelings I didn't know I still had for you.
Written in pen, in permanent ink, in the back of my notebook.

You are always a distant memory.
What we had.
What we could've had.
But it's over.

So, I tore out that page.
Set the page to flames.
That permanent ink destroyed.

I thought I was over you.
I thought.

I wrote out my feelings.
The feelings I had for you.
The feelings I can't get rid of.

I carved them into stone.
Chipping away at it.
Just as your actions chip away at my heart.
You hurt me.

I couldn't get over you.
You were always there.

You were.

I threw the stone into the ocean.
Open blue skies that collided with the blue sea.
The never-ending horizon that faded into sunset.

The stone.
A relic of what I felt for you.
Gone.

I wrote out an apology.
For the way I acted.
The way things ended.
An apology for me.
I wrote it on a napkin.
It may not be permanent,
but I meant everything I wrote.

Cinguomania

[sing-gyoo-loh-may-nee-uh]
noun

"A strong desire to hold a person in one's arms."

Heartbreak #1

Words.
　Empty and meaningless.
Even those meant for the strongest of feelings.
Their meanings meant to portray a deep bond.
An unbreakable bond.
But even the smallest of cracks can bring everything crumbling down.

Crashing and shattering,
Unable to be fixed.
Broken.
That bond that should have withstood storms and overcome mountains has crumbled.

And with it, a heart.
The heart of the vulnerable.
Not strong enough to withstand the possibility of a bad ending,
For they only believe in fairy tales.
Not reality.

Reality hurts.
It is not for the weak.
Yet, she was given a fake glimpse,
A glimpse of what she wants most.
Love.

Love Yourself Before Anyone Else

Without the possibility of heartbreak.
For it couldn't happen to her;
Right?
Wrong.

He put forth a fake mask.
Covering what he was capable of.
He could break her into a million pieces with few words.
For trust can get you anywhere.

The girl.
Now weak, broken, and more vulnerable,
Only wanting someone to be there for her.

So, when the destroyer shows back up,
Over
And over again,
She believes him when he says he has changed.

Empty apologies for his harm.
She is just a placeholder for him,
Someone to take up time before the next girl.

But to her, he is the entire world.
Perfection.
Could that be so far from the truth?

For she longs for one thing—
His love.
She knows it's fake.

Charley Johnson

She knows what he's capable of.
But she will do anything for the feeling of love again.

But broken love only breaks more.
She recovered what she could from the first heartbreak.
Just to be destroyed countless more times by the same boy.

He knows what he's doing.
He knows.
Love is a fantasy,
Unrealistic and harmful.
But after a glimpse of it,
You are stuck with the longing for more.

Love Yourself Before Anyone Else

Lust

noun

"A very strong sexual desire."

"He was motivated more by lust than love."

Heartbreak #2, What is Love?

Don't you hate it when you think you feel certain words,
But can't bring yourself to say them,

Afraid of scaring off the other person,
By saying them too early and ruining what could be?

When you have waited every time in the past,
But never quite got to that point before destruction.

Before everything came crashing down,
Because of your self-destruction.

When everything is confusing you,
And you can't help but overthink everything that crosses your mind.

So, you change your mind every minute,
Because you can't rid of the thought of the feeling.
But you fear the destruction coming again,
Because it happens every time.

You can't help it.
You try and try... but nothing.

No one seems to be able to prevent it,
Preventing the crashing of everything built,
The crumbling of every feeling created.

Charley Johnson

Induratize

Verb

"To make one's own heart hardened or resistant to someone's pleas or advances, or to the idea of love."

Meaning of Words

Words carry meaning.
Meanings of stone.
Piercing the flesh.
Hurting the bone.

Taking the hits.
They don't even know.
How much they break.
It doesn't show.

Mixed emotions.
Hurt or mad.
It damages your perception.
The one you had.

They replay in your head.
Over and over.
It makes you wish
that you weren't sober.

Words carry meaning.
And their hurt doesn't show.
Your words pierce my flesh.
More than you know.

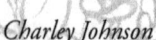

Charley Johnson

Tacenda

[ta-chen-da]

"Things better left unsaid; matters to be passed over in silence."

Things I Notice About You

The way you laugh.
The way you talk.
Things I notice about you.

The way you smile.
The way you walk.
Things I notice about you.

The way you make me feel.
The way I think of you.
Things I love about you.

The way you look at her.
The way she makes you smile.
Things I wish I didn't see.

You holding her hand.
You giving her love.
Things I wish I didn't see.

Your future with her.
No future with me.
Things I wish I didn't think about.

Charley Johnson

You used to look at me.
Now it's her.

Good morning and goodnight for her.
Love for her.

Movies, for her.
Hoodies, for her.

I see myself leaving the picture.
You have her now.
You leaving my life to become a part of hers.
The things I notice about you.

Viridity

Noun

"Naïve innocence."

Assume

"Two guys walked into a bar."
You think I'm going to tell a joke, right?
"He dribbles up to the net. Wide open court, steady hands."
You think he's going to shoot, right?
"The forecast says 90° and sunny skies."
Beautiful day to go to the beach, right?

I love how many assumptions are made in our daily lives.
People assume.
People assume that just because you are friends with a guy, you must like him.
Right?
Or that just because someone broke up with you, you're over them.
Right?
Or that you don't know how much you truly love someone until they are gone.
But that one is right.

You just assume they will stay forever because you love them.
You assume that they could never hurt you because of who they are.
You assume the best of them and nothing more.
You assume.

You assume but you are so far from the truth.
They can hurt you.
They can break you.
They can change you.
But you still feel the same about them.

You assume that it's not true.
That it can't be.
You assume.

You assume he can go back to who he was when y'all first met.
The guy who would FaceTime you all night with conversations that never stopped.
You assume that this won't last forever.
That he will love you again.

You assume that he didn't mean it.
That he will come back.
That everything will be ok.
Because he loves you,
Right?
You assume.

Fanna

noun

"Destruction of the self"

"Destroyed in love."

I'm Sorry I'm Texting Again

Sorry I'm texting again,
But have your ears been ringing.
Your name so sweet on my tongue I just want to say it.

I want to reach out to you and see how you are doing.
I hope you are doing better.
Seeing the world in colors,
Rather than black and white.

Sorry I'm texting again but I just wanted to know how your day was.
Did you eat today?
Was your food good?
Is my name still sweet in your mouth or has it turned bitter.

I'm sorry I'm texting again,
I just want to talk.
You're the first thought on my mind at every waking moment.
From the minute my eyes open until they shut again.
And even in my dreams,
There's no escape.

I don't think about food,

Charley Johnson

I try not to,
The thought of swallowing food makes my stomach turn.
But your name,
I want to call out,
I want to be heard.

I've grown used to seeing the words delivered by your name.
No longer seeing our smiling faces as I unlock my phone.

I'm sorry I'm texting again,
But you feel like home.
I feel safe talking to you,
I want to share everything.
But I feel like a bother,
When you reply with nothing.

I'm sorry I'm texting again,
I just wanted to talk to you.
I'll try to do it less.
Make my words very few.

I'm sorry I'm texting again.

Epiphany

[əˈpifənē]

"A moment when you suddenly feel that you understand. Or suddenly become conscious of something that is very important to you."

Nothing But a Seed

I could cry a rain shower,
And water a garden with my tears.
But nothing would grow,
Nothing to show.
Nothing to give to you my dear.

For salty tears and runny makeup
Can't make a flower bloom.
I can't treat them,
Keep them,
I just lead the seeds to their doom.

You gave me roses to plant,
With the hope that your flowers would forever bloom.
A never-ending cycle,
A daily reminder,
Of everything I have with you.

You gave me seeds to grow,
To show me how much you loved me.
But I can't grow flowers with tears,
So, we are nothing but a seed.

Reverie

['rev(ə)rē]

"A state of being pleasantly lost in one's thoughts; a daydream."

What "I Love You" Means

I love you stands for:

<u>I</u> can't get over you.
<u>L</u>onely without you, yet you made me feel so alone.
<u>O</u>ur love that we had, I can't stop reminding myself of it.
<u>V</u>isions of the future we could have had together, torn apart.
<u>E</u>very single moment you are on my mind, and it hurts.
<u>Y</u>ou were my first love.
<u>O</u>f course, I was the one that broke what we had.
<u>U</u>nbelievable that I do this every single time.

I miss us stands for:

<u>I</u> miss who you were.
<u>M</u>emories burned into my brain.
<u>I</u> can't stand the thought of you; it breaks me.
<u>S</u>o much time I had to become a better person.
<u>S</u>o much I could have done better.
<u>U</u>nbreakable, I thought, yet I was the one that broke everything.
<u>S</u>orry.

Goodbye stands for:

<u>G</u>et over him; it's been months.
<u>O</u>nly I could be this attached to a guy who wants nothing to do with me.
<u>O</u>ver time, I'll get over him, right?
<u>D</u>on't tell me this is it.
<u>B</u>elieve me when I say I've changed.
<u>Y</u>ou hurt me.
<u>E</u>ven though I believed you when you said you wouldn't.

I love you. And I miss us. But I guess this is goodbye.

Philophobia

"Fear of falling in love, getting into a relationship, or maintaining a relationship."

Blindly Led Off a Cliff

Loving you was my worst mistake.
I fell so hard, and you weren't there to catch me.
But why did I expect you to be?

In the beginning, you held my hand.
Led me by your side.
You were there.
Comforting me along the way.
I was so lost in your eyes that I didn't know where you were leading me.

Only when I was snapped back into reality,
When you left,
Did I realize where I was.

You led me to a cliff.
Standing on fragile stones.
One movement and it's my fate.

I was so lost in your fake love that I was led to danger.
Fooling me.
I thought I was safe with you.

Charley Johnson

I look over the cliff's edge,
Crying out for help.
I call your name.

After everything you did,
I want your help.

You show back up.
I'm relieved.
You're back.
You're different.
You love me.
Now.

Extending your arm.
I feel safe again.
A familiar feeling.
I forget about all the fear you brought me.
I forget how you tricked me the first time.

That wasn't you, right?
You're different now.
Right?

I go to grab your hand.
To be brought to safety.
You push.
You push me off the cliff.

Love Yourself Before Anyone Else

I was so vulnerable to you.
I was so willing to give up everything for your love.
I was blindsided.
And you led me to a cliff.

Filipendulous

[fil-i-pen-du-lous]
adjective

"Hanging by a thread."

By the Way...

I don't think about you anymore.
I know you don't care, but I thought you should know.

I don't obsess over dressing to impress you every day.
I don't try to act happier when I see your friends,
In hopes that they tell you I'm "doing great."

I don't scroll through our old messages.
Or look at our old photos.
Or think about the old us.

I don't care anymore.
Yes, some part of me does miss it.
But life goes on.
I have to accept that it's over.

You're gone.
You've moved on.
So, it's time I should.
I just thought you should know.

Anagapesis

[ana-ga-PE-sis]

"No longer feeling any affection for someone you once loved."

"Falling out of love."

My Body not my Heart

You ask for my body,
　To give you every piece of me.
You want to strip the clothes from my body,
So, it's my figure you see.

You want to kiss every inch of me,
Leave marks on my skin.
But it doesn't feel like love,
It feels like a sin.

Stripping the clothes from my figure,
As you stare in awe.
But you never cared about me,
Just what you saw.

You cared about my looks,
And when you called me beautiful it felt nice.
But that was the only time I felt secure with you.
Other than that, it was a fight.

I felt so comfortable with you,
that I didn't want to leave.
And when I ask if you care,
You say you want me.

Charley Johnson

But even though you want my body,
You exclude my heart.
It's not something you want to deal with.
It's not part of the "art."

It's something you'll look at,
But never touch.
It's too much to handle,
And you treat me as such.

You only care about me,
While we are doing something that pleases you.
But I want more than that,
And I don't know what to do.

I can't tell you I love you,
Because it's only my body you see.
You don't want anything more.
You don't want me.

You tell me you have needs,
But those needs are sex.
I have needs too,
But I guess my feelings are too complex.

Love Yourself Before Anyone Else

Xenization

noun

"The act of existing as a stranger."

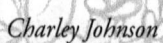

A Poem For You

Roses are red,
Violets are blue.
Do I still,
Have feelings for you?

I ask myself this daily.
But can never get to the truth.
I hide from my feelings,
and won't get down to the roots.

I won't uncover what I feel,
I just push it aside.
It doesn't even matter,
because it can't be right.

I can't love someone
who broke my heart.
But did they even
break it from the start?

Yes, it did hurt,
when he broke up with me.
But I never did hate him,
I just had some built -up steam.

Love Yourself Before Anyone Else

I didn't hate him,
I just regretted falling so hard.
I thought so far ahead,
When it crumbled, I broke my own heart.

I thought ahead to a future with you.
All of the things that we could do.
You were a good boyfriend,
I just wish things didn't end.

Roses are red,
Violets are blue.
I don't regret it.
I just wish I didn't still like you.

Charley Johnson

Cafuné

[ka-fu-ne]

"Running your fingers through the
hair of someone you love."

Our Story

The beginning of writing a book is always the hardest.
Everything slow.
Steady.
But it has to be.
It has to start.

You get to know the other person.
You start your chapter with him.

The book starts to speed up.
FaceTime calls.
Dates.
Movies.
It becomes real.

Midway through the book, he asks you to be his girlfriend.
A label.
The label you wanted.
Girlfriend.
But not just anyone's.
His.

He's the one you've always wanted.
But as the pages turn, it becomes familiar.
Hanging out.
Movies.

Kissing.
Texting.
Good morning.
Goodnight.
Repeat.

He gets bored.
Messaging slows.
He doesn't wanna hang out.
He's bored of you.

But you try to hold onto what you have.
Finding more pages to write your story.
There must be something new.
There has to be.

Our story can't just end.
I want there to be chapters.
Books.
Many books.
I don't want it to end.
Not now.

I go to turn the page.
But I'm stopped.
Hit with a message.
The one I've been dreading.

"This isn't working out.
I think we need time apart.

It's not your fault.
We just need… space."

Space.
But not the space between each written word.
Space.
Like you wish to start a new book.
A story with someone else.

But even if your story goes on,
I made sure to leave a blank page for you.
In case you ever felt like giving me another chance.
Then, I'll have space to go back and write.

Charley Johnson

Onsra

noun

"A bittersweet moment when you love for the last time or realize your love won't continue."

Live, Laugh, Love?

Live,
Laugh,
Love always being the second choice.

The one you go to when there's no other option.
The one that you know will always be there,
because I can't stand to leave you.

It hurts me when you go after other girls,
but I won't leave because I love you too much.

You crush any sort of expression of self-love,
because you want me to depend on you.

Depending on what you think of me,
and basing my attitude on how much affection I receive
from you.

Never looking for more because I am comfortable with
what I have.
I'm afraid of change,
and you know that.

Using that to use me as a safety net.
Someone you know will be there for you to go to.
Someone who won't leave, and you won't let free.

Charley Johnson

Thanatophobia

noun

"The phobia of losing someone you love."

Remember? Forget.

People forget.
Mostly unimportant things.
But sometimes not.

Things you should remember.
Things I wish you remembered.

Memories.
They fade over time.
You want to remember.
But they are clouded by new memories.

You don't want to think about it.
It hurts.
You can't have him anymore.
You want to remember.
But it only brings pain.

You forget.
You forget the way he made you feel.
The day you met.
The day he left.

The good memories of you and him fade.
Smiles.
Laughs.

Charley Johnson

Good nights.
Good mornings.
Love.

It all starts to disappear.
Like it never happened.
But it did.

You remember the bad things.
Arguments.
Fights.
The loneliness.
The isolation.
Him leaving.

It hurts to remember.
But you don't want to forget.

Wasted time.
You waste time waiting for him to come back.
You know he won't.
It's over.
He's moved on.
But you haven't.

You want to forget.
You need to move on.
But he's always there.
A memory.

You loved him.
More than you thought.
But you never got to tell him.
You never said, "I love you."

Regret.
You regret not saying it.
But you also regret falling so hard.
Especially when, in the end, he wasn't there to catch you.

He lifted her up.
Helping her off the ground.
As he pushed you down.
Reaching down as if to help you.
Only to laugh in your face.

You thought he was back.
You thought he was different.
You thought…

You think you want to remember.
But you need to forget.
The scar can't heal,
If you keep cutting it open.

Athazagoraphobia

noun

"The fear of forgetting, being forgotten
or ignored, or being replaced."

War of Nonsense

Trying to talk underwater,
Like trying to breathe with no air.
I talk, and I talk,
But all you do is stare.

Stare at me blankly,
Do you even hear my words?
You wait until I attack you,
Then you make it worse.

Using my words against me,
I can never win.
An endless war of nonsense,
That I didn't even begin.

I speak, you won't listen,
You never hear what I'm saying.
Please, just listen for once,
One time, I'm praying.

It's always my fault,
I can never have the upper hand.
You need to have control,
I don't know why; I don't understand.

Charley Johnson

I give you everything, every piece of me,
I ask about so little.
But every time I do,
You make it some sort of riddle.

You ignore me, change the topic,
Or turn my words around.
I can't have an opinion,
I can't make a sound.

I'm trying to talk to you,
Stop trying to make me drown.
I'm getting really tired,
Of keeping everything down.

Love Yourself Before Anyone Else

Anecdoche

noun

"A conversation in which everyone is
talking but nobody is listening."

Mr. No Name

Y ou were the talk of my group.
How good you treated me.
How we were going to last.
How we were perfect for each other.

You were the good example.
The example of the boyfriend they all wanted.

You've been replaced.
That position.
That role.
Someone else holds it now.

You are now known as the bad example.
The way none of them want a guy to make them feel.
Heartbroken.

You were a "nice boy."
The one my mom thought would treat her daughter right.
She trusted you as much as I did.
She liked you.
That doesn't happen often.

You met my dad.
My sister.
My brother.

My Grandma.

You were the "talk of the house,"
Because you made me happy.
You did.

You aren't mentioned anymore.
You aren't the good example.
You aren't you.
Mr. No Name.

Charley Johnson

Ilynga

"A person who will forgive anything the first time, tolerate it the second time, but never a third time."

Souls or Strings

Connected.
As if once soul mates
In another life.
Another time.

My words, they flow.
My trust, it shows.
I tell you everything.
Although it's you I hardly know.

Connected.
But not by strings.
Small bundles of rope,
that snap under tension.

I feel connected to you.
Our souls tied,
Not by the weakness of strings,
But the strength of iron.

Welded together.
No past.
Yet, a future?
Maybe.

You are different.
But I've fallen for this before.
I can only hope that you are different.
That this isn't a trap.

Falling too hard.
No one there to catch me.
Making the same mistake.
My mistake.

Letting my guard down.
I always regret it.
But I feel connected.
Our souls tied.

Connected by souls.
Not strings.

Love Yourself Before Anyone Else

Koi no yokan

[ko-ee no yo-kan]

"The extraordinary sense upon first meeting someone, that you will one day fall in love."

Before and After

The concept of love.
It is hard to explain.
But once you know the feeling.
It's always there.

Not the kind of love you feel towards your favorite food,
or a sport,
or a color.
Those are things you enjoy.
Things you like...
Not love.

You can't necessarily love an inanimate object.
But you can love a person.

Before you, I knew the love of family.
The way you love your mom and dad.
But it's not the love you feel toward a partner.

The butterflies you get when you hold their hand.
The longing for physical touch.
The longing for them...

The way you smile when they text.
Or spend hours on FaceTime.
The strong urge to say, "I love you."

Because you now know what it feels like…
Love.

Love.
It's the best thing to feel,
to understand.
But once you know the feeling you always want it,
Even when no one is there to give it to you.

You loved him,
but a bit too much.
You didn't think you could love someone too much until he left.

You don't receive his love anymore.
Now you are stuck with the longing for love.

Love is both a creator and a destroyer.
A creator of relationships…
A destroyer of a girl.
The want for love tears you apart.
You go after anyone willing to give it to you.

I want love,
but not from anyone.
From him.

Charley Johnson

Toska

noun

"Ache of soul; longing with nothing to long for."

The Balloon of Your Love

I miss our love,
The love we had.
Before you left,
When it went bad.

It once was full,
Full of air.
I was your one and only,
The one who was there.

There for you
through spikes and thorns.
You made me better,
Better than before.

You inflated my heart,
Made it full.
Full of joy and love
Like a shiny jewel.

You became distant,
Leaving my love behind.
My heart leaked,
You're still in my mind.

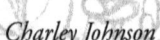

Charley Johnson

Deflating in size,
It no longer stood.
Sinking to the floor,
You were up to no good.

You know what you did,
Popping my love.
Unsalvageable, broken,
But I see you up above.

Floating away,
Up through the clouds.
No way to stop you,
To keep you around.

I hope you find love.
Someone to capture your heart.
I'll be okay,
Just watching you depart.

Floating away,
Up to the moon.
I did love you,
I just wish you didn't leave so soon.

Twitterpated

adjective

"Love-struck."

User Not Found

Added from quick add.
A simple request.
Deny or accept.
You know the rest.

I stare at my screen.
The quick push of a button.
You came into my life.
Made yourself important all of the sudden.

Day and night.
The conversations never ended.
I fell for you, I did.
All because it was me you friended.

We start to talk.
A simple word.
Something everyone does all day.
Just to be heard.

When I talk to you.
You stare at me and smile.
It makes me feel certain
You will stay for a while.

I put my trust in you.
I want something more.
You were just so perfect.
Who else could I be looking for.

It was you all along.
I say to myself.
So sure of it.
I knew that this is how I felt.

Talking became dating.
And hanging out some nights.
It seemed so easy. Effortless.
Without any fights.

Time went by.
You got used to me.
No need to for effort anymore.
You had me tucked beneath your sleeve.

I wasn't going anywhere.
I was now "yours."
There was no need for the long conversations,
I wanted before.

You don't seem to listen.
Yet, I still speak.
Unsure if I'm heard.
Your emotions so bleak.

User not found.
And a shattered heart.
Added from quick add.
Was only the start.

Love Yourself Before Anyone Else

Lyssamania

"The irrational fear that someone is upset with you; that although you did nothing wrong, your mind feeds into your insecurities, leaving you with more and more reasons to not accept that maybe people love you for who you are and nothing else."

Digging a Pit

Digging a hole.
Done with a shovel.
A thick piece of metal.
Makes the job easier.

Talking.
I talk to you.
You listen.
Do you reply?
Sometimes.

I try to get through to you.
Like digging through the ground.
Yet, it's not as easy as it sounds.
I think that I'm getting somewhere.
That you understand.
Word after word after word.
I tell you how I feel.
FIRST hand.

I explain that I need you to communicate with me.
To tell me how you feel.
You say, okay,
As if my feelings are no big deal.

In one ear out the other,
Is how I feel talking to you.
I talk and explain and try to get you to understand.
I just need you to let me get through.

I need you to listen.
And put in some effort.
Just a little effort.
Please.
I'm begging you here.
Because I'm trying to dig.
But you "don't wanna interfere."

You make up excuses,
So, we "don't have to fight."
But do you really want this?
Or am I just not right?

Not good enough for you.
Please, I'm trying really hard.
I just need you to communicate,
Like you did at the start.

I don't need a lot from you.
All that I ask.
Just, please, pick up the shovel.
So communication isn't a task.

Stardust

[stahr-duhst]

"A naively romantic quality."

Flow or Run

Water flows…
    But it also runs.
Like how the words flow from my mouth,
Yet, I can't confess my feelings for you.

I run from any expression of love,
Out of my own fear.
Fear that you will leave,
That you're like the rest.

Water freezes,
Becomes snow.
No two snowflakes alike.
Like people.

Yet I am so quick to assume.
Assume the worst,
Because that's all I've ever received.

Be different.
Be a snowflake,
And I will flow like the water from a faucet,
Not run like the water from a river.

Charley Johnson

Clysmic

adjective

"Cleansing, washing."

Roses

A bouquet of roses.
You claim, when the last rose dies, "us" is over.
Frantic,
I struggle to keep them alive.

Days go by,
Petals fall,
As do the tears from my eyes.

I can see the end.
But why?
Why put me through this?
Knowing when the end will come.

On the last day...
I sit,
Staring at the last rose.
One left standing.

The longer I look,
The more it starts to stand out.
All the petals intact.

I reach my hand out.
Soft fingers,
Rough petals?

Charley Johnson

Plastic.
The rose is plastic.

A bouquet full of roses,
The determiner of our love.
Flowers show love,
But they can't hold onto it.

I hold onto the fake rose,
The proof of our everlasting love.

Kalon

[ka-lon]
noun

"Beauty that is more than skin deep."

Can You Cry Underwater?

Blue as the sky,
My tears run.
Did you really love me?
Or was I just pointless fun?

Blue as the ocean,
The never-ending sea.
My tears for you,
Could drown you and me.

Crying you an ocean,
Because you're really gone.
Flooding my thoughts,
I feel I was in the wrong.

The reason you left,
Why you didn't stay.
I was the problem,
I was just in your way.

Crafting an ocean,
With my tears for you.
But you can't cry underwater,
So, then, it changes my view.

No more tears can run,
But I also can't breathe.
Because now that you're gone,
I'm suffocated by my self-made sea.

Charley Johnson

Orenda

(Huron)

"An internal summoning of personal strength to change fate; the courage to love someone against the obstacles life has set before you."

What You Want Me For

Seen through my eyes,
And seen through a lens.
Pulled into the mirror,
it's happening again.

Hey!
Hello!
Hi!
What do you look like?
How are you?
Wow, you're so pretty!
But I want to see what that body can do.

It's not about me.
Who I really am.
You just want to "add to your roster."
Just another option,
another fan.

But I want you still.
Even after all else.
Because even though you only want my body,
I still fell.

Charley Johnson

Fell for who you are,
or maybe who I imagined you to be.
Closing my eyes.
Making you the "perfect" guy for me.

Remember only the good.
What made you seem like "the guy."
Talking you up to everyone.
But it was all a lie.

I was so busy,
thinking ahead.
That you had all the time in the world,
to get me in your bed.
To use me for what you wanted.
To truly "finish your quest."
Because you got me to love you.
Just so I'd get undressed.

Love Yourself Before Anyone Else

Illecebrous

adjective

"Alluring, attractive, enticing."

A Poem Written When He Was Around

I look in your eyes.
Trapped in a trance.
Reflections of skies.
My figure and dance.

I could sit here forever.
Watching days pass through your view.
Beautiful sun rises and falls.
So much to do, but I only want you.

Here, even silence.
Just your presence is fine.
Close, near, or far.
I just want you to be mine.

Not to claim.
I don't need your name.
Just you will do.

You hold value,
Equal to gold.

Just to admire,
Not to be sold.

The safety of a hug.
Even just in thought.
Will protect me.
More than I've sought.

I'm not here to beg.
I'm not here to plead.
I don't want much.
Just you, I need.

Interpret how you shall.
I'll think my own way.
But I won't push.
I just want you to stay.

To watch the sun depart.
Through the view in your eyes.
Stay for a moment.
Not a goodbye.

Charley Johnson

Forelsket

[for-el-skit]

"The feeling of euphoria and infatuation when first falling in love."

Just Let Me Drown

It's getting hard again.
My own thoughts, my abuse.
Everything falling to pieces.
And I don't know what to do.

I don't want this to start.
It really hurts.
Why me?
What is it worth?

I can't stand the pain.
It really stings.
Anger floods my voice.
I say stupid things.

I can't handle this again.
Please I need help.
This isn't a cry for him.
It's a scream of how it's felt.

How it feels to fall apart.
Please, I'm breaking again.
I don't mean to hurt you.
I just need a hand.

Charley Johnson

I'm drowning in tears.
I let the thoughts win.
It's gunna all go to hell.
When I start old habits again.

The silver, it calls.
And it won't be silenced.
But you don't need to worry.
This time, I'll keep it private.

To not burden those around me with my really dark thoughts.
Don't worry,
I'm okay.
Just a bit distraught.

The silver will heal,
My messed-up head.
Don't worry about me.
Just go to bed.

I won't sleep.
Not tonight.
But maybe at some point,
I'll be alright.

It's happening again.
I'm breaking down.
But don't try to save me.
Just let me drown.

Lisztomania

noun

"A need to listen to music all the time."

My Friend, Jim

In life, you choose your friends.
Who you hang around.
Who you want to be around.
But what about the friend that never leaves my side?
Let's call him Jim for now.

Jim is always there.
Whether I know it or not.
He keeps me up at night.
Making me put up a fight.

He reminds me of my faults.
And drains my every day.
I try to ignore him.
But he just won't go away.

The longer Jim is around.
The better he gets at his job.
Taking my motivation to do anything worth my time.
I just want to sit and sob.

Even things I should be doing.
Something simple for someone else.
Like waking up in the morning,
Is now a task.

Jim just sits on top of my chest.
Like a heavy weight.
Telling me to stay in bed.
And that I shouldn't be awake.

In life, you should be able to choose your friends.
Not be stuck with them.
But Jim just showed up.
He's not something I condemn.

His real name?
Depression.
And he's here to stay.
I guess I just have to accept it and move on.
Because Jim,
My depression,
Will never go away.

L'appel du Vide

("the call of the void")

"A French phrase used to refer to intellectual suicidal thoughts, or the urge to engage in self-destructive (suicidal) behaviors during everyday life."

Grey Skies

The pretty blue sky,
Fades into grey.
Oh, but the colors were pretty.
I wish they would stay.

I look in the mirror,
And I try to see
Where the little girl went.
What happened to me?

I notice it more
With each passing day.
I've changed a lot.
It's hard to dismay.

The little girl I was,
Who wore bright colorful shirts.
Won't leave the dark hoodies.
And it really hurts.

It hurts to see the color
Drained from my soul.
I've been through so much.
It's really taken a toll.

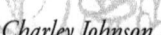

Charley Johnson

I'm not who I was.
I mean, how could I be?
The same smiley girl
Just isn't me.

I fake who I am,
Just to seem okay.
I'm really not, though.
It hurts more than I say.

I smile and act
Like that sweet happy girl.
The one that I was,
Who brightened everyone's world.

Who made it her goal
To always be okay.
What happened to her?
When did she go astray?

The red from my lips,
That shows when I smile.
The red on my wrists
Will hurt for a while.

The colors, the meanings,
They aren't the same.
I smile on my face,
While hiding so much pain.

Love Yourself Before Anyone Else

I want to be happy.
I really do.
It's just hard to see the color
When it's grey skies, not blue.

Charley Johnson

Desiderium

"An ardent longing, as for something lost."

I'm Not Perfect

Perfection.
I am the farthest from it.
But you see me differently.

I am pretty in your eyes.
But I only see your compliments as petty.

You must feel bad for me.
That's why you compliment.
There is so much I would change.
How could *I* be perfect?

I pick apart my body.
Finding every
single
thing
wrong with me.

How do you not see it?
My insecurities.

You must.
They stand out.
They are loud.
They scream "different."
I don't wanna be different.
I wanna be perfect.

Charley Johnson

Atelophobia

noun

"Fear of imperfection."

Poetry is Love

The silence surrounds me.
The pencil tip glides.
An escape from the world.
Something to clear my mind.

Poetry is an escape.
An escape from reality.
Poetry is freedom.

My words come alive.
Thoughts dancing in my head.
Spinning and spiraling,
Thinking of so many things to write next.

Poetry is comforting,
like a warm gentle hug.
It wraps me in its arms,
and it doesn't give up.
It won't let me down.
It doesn't go away.
Short lines or full sentences,
to rhyme or to not.
I can decide.
I have control.

Charley Johnson

I have control over what I write.
Control.

Control brings stability.
A little peace to my life.
While having control over very little.
I know I can write.

Letting my words flow.
I can express my thoughts.
Speak the truth.
Speak from the heart.

The paper won't judge.
The paper won't shame.
The paper feels like home.
It is safe.

I love poetry.
It knows me the most.
Keeping my feelings safe.
Poetry is an escape.

Fustian

noun

"Pretentious writing or speech."

More Than My Writing

I write what I think.
In my dark empty mind.
But what about the small portion,
The things I leave behind.

The things that I love.
That make me, me.
Like writing,
Or lifting,
Or fishing the sea.

I don't like emotions,
So, "happy" just isn't there.
I give it no devotion.
It's nothing I share.

I don't share how I love flowers.
To draw or to see.
Pink.
Red.
White.
They seem so free.

Each so individually different.
Like the people I love,
My friends who care.
And would hate to see me up above.

I love the sun
When it dips below the shore.
Where the water meets the sky.
A view I adore.

My depression eats me away.
But there are things I save.

My memories of traveling.
Of seeing it all.
Something I crave to do.
And I always recall.

I may be a lot.
And I may be broken.
But I do have things I love.
That should be spoken.

My love for the simple things.
That I have in my life.
Flowers.
Sunsets.
Writing.
Something more than a knife.

Charley Johnson

My thoughts may be dark.
And with that, my writing.
But I am more than I say.
And more than you portray.

Pulchritudinous

[pul-chri-tude]
noun

"Possessing beauty that is breathtaking or heartbreaking."

Can I Succeed?

I lay on my floor,
Paralyzed in my skin.
Trapped in my mind,
My patience gone thin.

Life is tiring,
Day in and day out.
I just need a break,
To not deal with doubt.

Doubting myself,
and what I've become.
Doubt from others,
and just feeling numb.

I don't know what I want,
Or what I really need.
I don't have emotions,
And I don't care if I succeed.

Succeed in school,
Or life in all.
I don't care anymore,
It's too much to haul.

To carry around,
I feel trapped in my bed.
Weighed down by depression,
I get in my head.

I don't know what I feel,
Yet, I feel so weak.
So helpless.
My emotions so bleak.

I'm sorry for those
Who have crossed my path and more.
I'm not a good person,
Even if I had been before.

I drag myself down,
And others with me.
I can't save you from drowning,
When I also can't breathe.

I want to help you,
But I'm not enough.
I put forth an act,
The smile is a bluff.

I'm stuck in my body,
And I don't know what to be.
It's hard to see a future for yourself,
When failure is all you see.

Charley Johnson

Egonoia

Egomania + paranoia

"The fear of people being annoyed by you or talking about you in an unrealistically negative light, typically due to self-obsession, insecurity and/or self-dysmorphia."

Just Cry

Bottle it up.
Keep it that way.
Don't show your emotions.
It's your price to pay.

It helps with absolutely nothing.
It does you no good.
Push it down.
And be happy like you should.

I took that too literally.
Never showing how I feel.
I don't know how to anymore.
I don't know how to deal.

How to deal with myself.
Even when I break down.
I don't know how to cry.
Even if no one is around.

I just want to cry.
Tears running down my face.
To just let it all out.
To just embrace.

Charley Johnson

Embrace the emotions.
I just want to feel.
Feel anything for that matter.
Just to feel real.

I never feel good.
Nor do I feel bad.
I don't feel happy.
I don't feel sad.

I don't feel joy or sorrow or pain or love.
I wish I could.
I just want to feel human.
I just want to feel good.

To want to be myself.
To love me for me.
But when I look in the mirror.
I don't know who I see.

I don't know who I am.
Or who I want to be.
I don't see a future for myself.
I just want to breathe.

To be told I'm enough.
Just a hug would be nice.
I feel like I'm just surviving.
Not loving life.

Love Yourself Before Anyone Else

I want to be okay.
And I just want to cry.
But I'm not able to.
And I blame myself for why.

Charley Johnson

Tears

noun

"The blood of the soul. When the soul bleeds, you cry."

Make a Wish

I'd tear out all of my lashes,
If you asked for a wish to blow.
A good luck charm, even with harm,
But I want you to know.

Know I care, I love you dear,
I'd do myself any harm.
I'd give you the entire world,
I'd be your good luck charm.

I'd give you my last penny,
All of the money that I made.
For you to toss into a fountain,
Just so you will stay.

I want all your dreams to come true,
I'd help at any cost.
I'd be the light in front of you,
So, you never would be lost.

Do you want to make a wish?
I'll give you everything you ask.
I don't want anything in return,
I just want the moment to last.

Charley Johnson

Lachrymose

[lach-ry-mose]

"Tearful or given into tears."

Vocal Cords

Grab me by the throat.
Make me listen to you.
You're right. I'm wrong.
There's nothing I can do.

You ask for an answer,
a reply, to admit.
Admit I'm wrong and you're right.
If I don't, you'll throw a fit.

Rip the vocal cords from my throat.
You won't let me respond.
If it's not the words you want to hear,
Then, they are just flat-out wrong.

You're right, I'm wrong,
That's the only way it can be.
My feelings are invisible to you.
Why can't you just see?

See how you make me feel.
Your words pierce my skin.
I wish I could explain this to you,
But I don't know where to begin.

Charley Johnson

Even if I tried,
You'd shove my feelings down.
Every time I say how I feel,
You make me feel like a clown.

Like all I do is overreact.
I'm dramatic; I'm wrong.
How can I love you,
When you make me feel like I don't belong?

How can we have a conversation,
One that goes both ways,
When you rip my vocals out?
But I apologize, anyway.

Love Yourself Before Anyone Else

Agathokakological

"Composed of both good and evil"

Bloody Hands

You tore my heart from my chest,
But I'm sorry for your bloody hands.
What a mess you have to clean.
I'll never understand.

You might have shattered me in pieces,
But it got everywhere.
I'm sorry for the inconvenience.
I'll clean it up, I swear.

I'm sorry, I'm sorry, I'm sorry, I'm sorry.
Please, forgive me now.
I know you lied and manipulated me.
But I didn't throw in the towel.

I stuck around; it's my fault.
I could have just left.
I tried to fix things over and over,
I caused my own stress.

Believing in the make-believe,
I tried to understand.
So, when you tore my heart out,
I washed your bloody hands.

Bêtise

"An act of foolishness or stupidity"

Patience With Love

Peace and well-being,
not easily obtained.
For the boundaries placed before us,
we strive to strain.

Pleading for love,
to love and be loved by someone else.
Without possessing the knowledge,
of how to love ourselves.

Love is not known,
for there is not one kind.
Our souls are tied to another's,
Which we will find.

The person to give your love to,
and to love you must meet their needs.
There is no defining how we love,
it's simply being able to please.

Pleasing your partner and pleasing yourself,
For love is not easily attained.
And if you think it is,
it's what love is,
You may have strained.

Blinded by what you believe to be love,
But you'll surely know it when it arrives.
You'll bask in their presence,
your peace and well-being will thrive.

Peace and well-being,
not easy to acquire.
You must learn your goals in life,
And patience with love, you must aspire.

Charley Johnson

Redamancy

noun

"The act of loving the one who loves you; a love returned in full."

Your Love 2 – Self Love

When I sit in silence,
I recall my past,
Remembering when I was weak,
Vulnerable because of love.

Our love didn't last,
And that, I could not accept.
Like many other aspects of my life,
Reality was not "real."

It was all just a dream.
Something behind the lids of my eyes.
Or more like a nightmare,
Your absence bringing dark skies.

But I fear the dark,
And being alone.
So, each time you hurt me,
Shut me out,
I looked for the light.
Your light.

Something good,
So I could oversee your bad.

Charley Johnson

But the more I lit your candle,
The shorter that it last.

Trying to shield the flame.
The little bit of light.
Willing to give everything…
My dignity,
Just so we wouldn't fight.

My nightstand littered with lighters.
Just so I was prepared.
To light your flame,
To see the good.
It was my priority.

Love should be equal.
I know that now.
50/50
Not 90/10
Two fragrances.

When your candle broke,
And our love was destroyed,
It was my mission,
To savor the memories.

To not forget.
Because I felt empty without you.
But after a while,
I could not remember your smell.

Love Yourself Before Anyone Else

The scent of your candle.
The smell of your love.

In the absence of your candle,
A new scent arose.
One familiar, yet subtle,
And still unknown.

As I focused on myself,
And healed from my past,
I realized the new aroma,
Was my own candle, at last.

Charley Johnson

Agape

|a-ga-pe|
noun

"The highest form of love. Selfless, sacrificial, and unconditional love; persists no matter the circumstance."

What Is Love?

Love

noun

"A person you have a deep affection for. Someone you will allow to put their cold feet on your warm legs."

Love

"Love is our moral character, and we can show it by the way we act and treat other people."

Love

/luhv/ (*noun*)

"Love is patient, love is kind. It does not envy, it does not boast, it is not proud. It is not rude; it is not self-seeking; it is not easily angered; it keeps no record of wrongs. Love does not delight in evil but rejoices with the truth. It always protects, always trusts, always hopes, always perseveres. Love never fails."
Corinthians 13: 4-8

Love

(*noun*)

"Giving them the last piece of cake, no matter how much you want it."

Self-Love
noun
"Nurturing your mind, body, and soul. Embracing experiences that shape you. Looking in the mirror and knowing you are worthy, you are capable, you are beautiful."

Self-Love
/self-luhv/ (*noun*)
"Being in love with every part of yourself. Taking care of your own needs and not sacrificing your well-being to please others. Not settling for less than you deserve."

Self-Love
"It's not something you acquire. It's always been there, and it never left. Waiting for you to shed your layers of identification with the thoughts of your mind and return back home. The greatest love story ever told. Yours."

Explore My Other Work
Shine Light on Mental Fights

The majestic creature we know as the butterfly may not be large in size, but it is large and in meaning. From birth to caterpillar, to the formation of its cocoon. From the first subtle movements of the butterfly's fragile wings, it holds important meaning. The butterfly holds the representation of hope, change, transformation, spiritual rebirth, and life. Like the butterfly, we all have the ability to transform ourselves into the better version of us that we strive to become.

We all have a story, which comes with its struggles to shape us. However, we fail to recognize the severity of many of those struggles. The struggles in which our mind is our biggest enemy. Fighting our own thoughts, feeling alone in this endless battle we call life. But you are not alone. We all face similar hardships, and no one should be ashamed of reaching out for help. Sometimes that shoulder to lean on will make the biggest difference in your day-to-day life. This is a book of poems to understand and relate to the biggest mental illnesses many young adults suffer from in today's society. A book of meaningful rhymes to relate to your hard times.

Follow me on Instagram: @johnsonbooks26

www.ingramcontent.com/pod-product-compliance
Lightning Source LLC
Chambersburg PA
CBHW070546090426
42735CB00013B/3083